WHO IS
PADRE PIO?

The photographs used in this pamphlet are inserted with the permission of the copyright owner, Federico Abresch of San Giovanni Rotondo, Foggia, Italy.

TAN BOOKS AND PUBLISHERS, INC.
Rockford, Illinois 61105

Imprimatur:

✠ Joannes Gregorius Murray
   Archiepiscopus Sancti Pauli.
   Paulopoli die 27a Julii 1955.

Translation by Laura Chanler White

Originally published by

Fathers Rumble and Carty
Radio Replies Press, Inc.
St. Paul, Minn., U.S.A.

Complete and Unabridged

ISBN 0-89555-101-2

TAN BOOKS AND PUBLISHERS, INC.
P.O. Box 424
Rockford, Illinois 61105

1974

WHO IS PADRE PIO?

Never forget that in the hospital are also those who are dying.

O. Guarini

PREFACE

In writing this little book my object is to spread knowledge of Padre Pio of Pietrelcina, of the Capuchin Fathers, increasingly all over the world.

In a few pages the reader should be able to get some idea of this son of St. Francis of Assisi, who so much resembles the apostle of charity.

Unfortunately, the tumultuous existence that we lead interferes with reading large volumes; we are driven by too many occupations and interests and are obliged to take advantage of the merest fractions of our free time, which we often use in far different ways than in the renewal of our spiritual life.

Many people have complained to me by word of mouth or in writing that they were unable to read my books: "Per la Storia," "Fino alla Meta," and "Fatti Nuova," because of their cost, or from lack of time.

I believe that these difficulties have been eliminated with the publication of this little volume, and I hope that these same people will now be able to form an adequate picture in their minds of the Reverend Padre Pio of Pietrelcina. If as a result they feel the desire to know this messenger of love better, try by all means to go to him. This may of course be impossible, because of a question of health or money. So the next best course is to read all that has been written about him, so that they may become familiar with this man of God who has been sent to us in this critical moment of the world's history.

They, too, will learn to "believe" in the fullest meaning of the word, since believing in a mystery truly admits of no limitations and no compromises with one's intellect, for if it did, we would be merely philosophizing.

In order to believe, however, it is essential to want to believe, and whoever goes to the Father with this intention will acquire courage for the fullness of life; living consists not only of Faith, but also of Hope and of Charity.

It is in the name of these three virtues that I am writing these pages, and whatever profit I make of them will be turned over to the "House for the Relief of Suffering," the magnificent hospital that was built by the Father in order to minister to the sufferings of the very poorest.

I declare, as I always do, that in obedience to the decrees of the Sovereign Pontiffs, I recount these facts with purely human credibility, having recourse to the prescriptions of the Church, our only Mother and Teacher.

THE AUTHOR.

BIOGRAPHY

To tell of the Reverend Padre Pio of Pietrelcina is the easiest as well as the most difficult of tasks; it is easy since his life is like an open book in which all may read, but hard in that the impression received by each one who sees him is hardly ever the same as the next man's. These impressions are varied and complicated, according to the state of grace, the condition of conscience, the personality of the visitor.

Who is this Padre Pio? Many people have wondered hearing him spoken of so often.

I shall begin by saying that he is a very humble Capuchin who wears the habit of St. Francis of Assisi. He was born on May 25th, 1887, of poor country people, at Pietrelcina in the Province of Benevento. His father, who was called Zi'Orazio (Uncle Orazio) by everyone, died on the 7th of October 1946 and is buried with his wife Giuseppa who died some years earlier, at San Giovanni Rotondo. Their tomb is visited by all pilgrims who come to see the Padre.

Padre Pio was born of parents who were poor in material things but rich in matters of the spirit, for they had a deep love and respect for our holy religion. He was baptized Francesco Forgione, and grew up in Pietrelcina. He was different from his contemporaries in that he did not share in the wild games and adventures or the strife of the other boys. From his earliest childhood he showed a kind of recollection of spirit and a love for the things of God, seeing Him in the beauty of the clouds and the stars and loving to hear of his goodness.

This awareness of God brings with it a sort of change in focus on the world and in his case, developed a profound conception of justice, discrimination of good and evil, of the pure and the impure. At the same time it implanted in his soul a

3

grace and gentleness that led him toward the goal that he had set himself, which was to perfect his nature and live ever more in harmony with his ideals.

In spite of this, the little peasant boy took part in the rural festivities and the simple life of his family. When the grown-ups danced or beat out the grain on the threshing floor of their houses and the children played about their mothers' skirts, or when the bigger boys were teasing each other with practical jokes, little Francesco, who had surely never heard of the Canticle of the Sun, was expressing the same ideas in his own words when he praised God and Mother Earth and his brother the Sun, all of the natural beauty surrounding him and filling him with joy.

From a very inadequate private tutor he received the first instructions in reading and arithmetic, but this poor man was able to teach him little. Family gossips blamed the pupil rather than the teacher for the little progress that was made, but they were wrong, for as soon as the boy was entrusted to another teacher, a certain Caccavo, with whom he remained until he was fourteen, litle Francesco immediately showed a lively intelligence.

In 1902 his father entered him in the monastery of Morcone where he was to prepare for the novitiate. His superior was extremely severe with him, and Padre Pio admits to never having seen the countryside when walking about with his classmates, as they were all obliged to keep their eyes fixed on the ground.

It was at this time that he began his severe penances and fasting. When his parents went to see him, they found him so emaciated and run-down that they tried to take him home. The Father Provincial, however, having sensed a quality in his young pupil that distinguished him from the others, persuaded the parents to leave him.

From Marcone he went to Sant'Elia in Panisi, and then to Venafro, where he lived for twenty-one days with the sacred host as his sole nourishment. In spite of his fasting he had gained weight, and when Zi'Orazio came to see him a year later he was pleased with his appearance.

After this he was transferred to Serra Capriola, to Montefusco, and to other places, where he continued his advance on the road to perfection through penance, fasting and prayer.

Whereas Our Lord was well pleased with his new servant, Satan, the spirit of Evil, seeing that this most desirable prey was evading him, proceeded to tempt him with unprecedented variety and violence.

Whenever he was forced by his poor health to seek a little change, he came back to Pietrelcina and his father's house.

He was once advised to take off his monk's habit and become a secular priest, but he refused, not wishing to be unfaithful to St. Francis.

One day as he was walking with the Pastor of the village, when they had reached the open country he suddenly stopped and became rapt in a kind of trance while listening to the ringing of distant church bells.

"What is the matter with you?" asked Don Salvatore.

"Nothing," he answered, "but the sound of those bells reminds me of bells of the vanished monastery; it will some day be here again, and larger and more beautiful than before!"

It seemed to him that he was hearing a chorus of angels giving praise to the Lord, and he added: "I don't know when this will come about, but it will."

It happened that in June 1947, His Excellency Msgr. Manginelli, Bishop of Benevento, did consecrate in Pietrelcina a monastery of the Capuchin Fathers. It had been endowed twenty years earlier by a spiritual daughter and convert of Padre Pio's, a well-to-do American lady, Miss Mary Pyle.

In this same monastery on the 20th of September, 1947, being the thirtieth anniversary of the appearance of the stigmata on the Padre, some of his spiritual children presented him with a ciborium and some vestments.

The dream of the young novice had become a reality.

However, before all these things were to happen, he had to go through much suffering and many disappointments; his pallor betrayed to many that he had the disease that can not be ignored, tuberculosis.

However, the infinite mercy of God never disappoints those who place in Him all of their confidence, and the Padre had more than once told himself: "Oh Lord, I have done your will!" He knew, besides, that suffering was the surest way for God to enter his soul and never leave it.

Padre Pio knew well that in order to receive one must give, and he gave all of himself. The only complaint ever to pass his lips was that he had not given enough and had received too much.

HIS ORDINATION

On the 10th of August, 1910, Padre Pio was ordained in the Cathedral of Benevento. The city had once been named "Maleventum" or Evil Wind by its founder Diomede, because of the violent winds that prevail there, but the Romans renamed it Beneventum, or Good Wind.

The higher the Padre mounted up the scale of perfection, the more fiercely did Satan attack him. One night he saw his bed surrounded by the most fearful monsters who shouted to him: "See, the Saint is retiring!"

"Yes, in spite of you!" he answered; and was promptly seized, shaken and beaten to the ground.

The more he was tormented by the Devil, the greater grew his faith and his love for Our Lord.

Another time, when he was ill in bed, he saw a friar come into his cell who looked like his former confessor, Father Agostino. The apparition proceeded to advise him to give up his practise of penance, of which God did not approve. Padre Pio, much astonished, ordered his visitor to call out: "Viva Gesù!" The strange creature disappeared, leaving behind a strong smell of sulphur.

He had many of these supernatural manifestations, and has had many since, but it would take too long to describe even the most startling of them.

During this period, the good Father Agostino, although getting on in years, continued to follow the career of his much-loved disciple and kept up a lively correspondence with him. When our holy Mother the Church comes to permit the publication of these letters, it will be possible to learn about the mysterious attacks that the poor Father has undergone from his terrible and invisible enemies. In the meantime he was ordered by the Archpriest to give over the unopened letters to him, without having read them.

One day a letter came to Padre Pio from Father Agostino, whose writing he recognized; he took it to the Archpriest who, having opened it, found a plain sheet of paper with no writing on it. "The good father must have forgotten to write anything," he said, "or else he just put a sheet of paper in the envelope instead of the letter."

"No," answered Padre Pio, "he did not forget, it is 'those gentlemen' who want to play me their usual trick."

"What do you know about it?"

"I know . . . "

"You think so! Then you will no doubt be able to tell me what was in the letter?"

"Most certainly!" and he proceeded to tell him exactly what Father Agostino had written to him.

The Archpriest, not believing Padre Pio, wrote to Father Agostino and his answer confirmed the truth as it had been told him.

Many things of this sort happened to him and others besides, but it would take too long to tell of them. The most notable grace, however, that he received from Almighty God was that of the Stigmata.

THE STIGMATA

Padre Pio first received the invisible Stigmata in Pietrelcina on the 20th of September 1915, and the visible ones at San Giovanni Rotondo on the same date in 1918. This did not happen in the case of the seventy other stigmatists that the Church has so far canonized. Gemma Galgani is the latest of these to be so honored.

Much could be said on the subject of this supernatural gift with which Padre Pio has been blessed by Divine Providence, but I, for one, am too ignorant not only to explain the gift, but to discuss its nature. I shall only say that the invisible Stigmata came to him while he was in the garden or orchard of his home in Pietrelcina, on a morning in September in the year 1915.

Only his confessor, Don Salvatore Panullo, is in a position to know the whole story, and his account of it has been transmitted to Rome and placed in the safe-keeping of Our Holy Mother the Church. We know that on that day, Padre Pio began his ascent of Mount Tabor, the scene of the Transfiguration. Since Our Lord was his model, and he was in a state of grace, God gave him this sign of His love which he had received through hardship and suffering accepted for His Divine Son and offered to Him.

God became man in Christ, to suffer for men and among men, and Padre Pio, being a man, imitated Christ, the Divine Master. The Capuchin had been more than once heard to repeat the sublime words: "Father in Heaven, do with me what you will, not what I will!"

But on Friday, the 20th of September 1918, there happened to him an event that not only changed his whole life, but that singled him out from the rest of humanity. He was praying in his stall in the choir when suddenly the monks heard a piercing cry. On running to find the cause of it they came upon Padre Pio lying unconscious on the floor of the choir, his hands, his feet and his side marked with deep, bleeding wounds. He was carried to his cell where he gradually recovered consciousness, begging his brothers to keep his secret. He had worn invisible stigmata for three years, and now they were there for all to see. They have remained the same until this day. He has been the subject of endless and often painful medical examinations, and has undergone every kind of supposedly healing treatment, but the wounds remain open and completely free from infection. He loses about a cupful of blood every day from his side, which is covered at all times with a linen cloth to prevent the endless staining of his garments. He wears brown half gloves on his hands excepting when he is saying mass. Nobody knows how much Padre Pio suffers from his wounds, but his rather halting gait is evidence enough of his constant awareness of his transpierced feet. When asked if the stigmata were painful, he laughingly replied: "Do you think that the Lord gave them to me for a decoration?"

I shall not dwell upon the manner in which the news spread like lightning all over the village, the Puglie, the Continent of Europe, and finally the whole world.

Padre Pio is the first priest ever to have received the Stigmata, for St. Francis was not a priest.

As I have said, the whole world began to hear of this wonder, and our Holy Mother the Church, ever prudent, ordered that the facts be examined by scientific methods.

The first person to be sent there to make a report, was Doctor Luigi Romanelli of Barletta. After five visits he felt obliged to state that he: "had been unable to discover a scientific explanation that would authorize him to classify such wounds."

This was a positive statement, but also full of spiritual meaning, as it declared science to be beyond its depth, and unable to explain the circumstances or the facts.

The newspapers sent their correspondents, who were in a great state of bewilderment, but who, all of them, whether willing or no, were forced to admit the truth of what they saw.

From that time San Giovanni Rotondo became the objective of pious pilgrimages. People came to the Father to beg his help and intercession with the God of all Love. The good that the Father has accomplished until now is known only to God, who has it written in His great book, for men are not always grateful. Although there are plenty who openly declare and confirm in writing the miracles or graces they have obtained, there are others who, having gotten what they were so ardently longing for, no longer wish to hear Padre Pio spoken of, and claim that things would have turned out that way anyhow, without his prayers.

These are the ones that I am most sorry for, more than for any atheist who does not believe and for one who does not see, for these do not wish to believe although they have seen. They are the unfortunate ones, like a certain Roman professor who, although he had seen the truth with his own eyes, did not wish to recognize it, and repented too late.

The Vatican sent both Professor Bignami of the University of Rome and Professor Giorgio Festa, also of Rome, but without either one knowing of the other's visit. Whereas the first was violently opposed to the Church the other was a good Catholic, and took the completely opposite side in the discussion. When Professor Festa discovered that his account was entirely different from that of Professor Bignami, he was seized with doubts and scruples, fearing that he had been mistaken in his observation. He went back several times to revisit Padre Pio, only to be convinced after most meticulous examinations, that he had made no mistakes. This led him to declare that the five lesions observed by him corresponded to: "The five parts of His body that Our Lord offered up in His supreme Holocaust to faith," adding that "They can only constitute a mystery for those who are unable to see a connection between natural truths and those of faith and religion."

Thomas à Kempis, in the Imitation of Christ, says: "Worldly honors have always Sorrow for company," and these words are written on the door of cell No. 5 which was occupied by Padre Pio in the monastery of Santa Maria delle Grazie in San Giovanni Rotondo. He now occupies cell No. 1. These honors have indeed brought sorrow to Padre Pio, for he has been visited by men of every sect, and of the most varied religious and philosophical beliefs who have published the wildest fictions and most unlikely stories about him, whereas he offered himself all to God and imitated His Divine Son more closely every day.

He returned good for evil, especially in the case of those who had offended him the most, and I admit to being myself one of these.

I was once a Mason, a despiser of priests, of nuns and of

11

saints. In Florence in 1919, I wrote libelous articles against Padre Pio in the anticlerical newspaper "L'Italia Laica" when I knew him only by name.

God punished me, and I thank Him for that punishment, since it allowed me to change my opinions in time, and save my soul. In November 1930, I went for the first time to see the Father, more out of curiosity than conviction, and in the presence of that extraordinary personality I was able in my inmost being to realize how wrong I had been and to utter a hymn of praise and of thanksgiving to God. I had so often been guilty of blasphemy, and now He was allowing me to see the Light, that Light that has ever since shone on the road that I travel, and that, please God, will continue to do so for the rest of my life.

The atheist in me had been overcome, and Satan had undergone another defeat; the first fruits of love and of faith began to grow along my path

I do not know how all this came about; there exist indescribable conditions in the human soul, probably in our subconscious mind but nonetheless guided by reason as well as feelings. They are like a beneficent rain that comes to a parched land; like a dazzling light that prevents us from seeing at first by what we are surrounded; like a familiar song from a distant homeland, like the gentle talk of a mother and child.

We feel these things in ourselves and are unable to explain or describe them, they make us laugh and sing and long to tell the whole world of our joy, of our love, of this wonderful melody that intoxicates us and that only a genius can express through the medium of art. It is the true poetry of life, that Dante immortalized in his verse, Michelangelo in his sculpture, Raphael in his painting and Chopin in his music.

12

It is something so wonderful that we cannot keep it to ourselves, for it bursts out, breaking all bonds and throwing
everyone and everything into confusion; we feel that we
simply must tell the world of our happiness.

"Credo, credo, credo!" that was the word that I kept re
peating when I saw Padre Pio for the first time. Today my
Credo is more perfect, for I say: "Christ, I believe in Thee,
the ultimate good. Thou only art the King of Kings, I adore
and worship only Thee."

THE SUPERNATURAL GIFTS OF PADRE PIO

It has been erroneously stated that the spiritual children of
Padre Pio are fanatics, because they love him too much. This
is not true; they love the Padre because he brings them
nearer to God — they love him just for that.

You must not forget that if it is true that the Padre is the
first stigmatized priest of the Church, he is also the only
known living priest who has the gift of perfume, of conversion, of bilocation, of discernment of spirits; and of pene-
trating the future.

Other saints have had the gift of perfume, e.g. St. Theresa,
St. Dominic, St. John of the Cross, St. Catherine of Genoa,
St. Rita of Cascia, St. Frances of Rome, St. Francis of Paul,
St. Clare of Assisi, and others. There have been many saints
who could exercise the power of conversion; the Church has
been rich in these.

There have been saints who cured the sick and the infirm,
and those who had the gift of bilocation like St. Anthony of
Padua, St. Alphonsus of Liguori, St. Alma, St. Malgondus,
St. Bridget, St. Dominic Guzman, St. Rita of Cascia, St.
Theresa of Avila. Certain saints had the gift of the discern-
ment of spirits like St. Joseph of Cupertino, St. Frances of
Rome, Blessed Anna Maria Taigi and Don Vincenzo Palotti.

There have been saints who prophesied like St. Lawrence Cipriano, St. Perpetua, St. Saturus, St. Hildegarde and others, but not one of them had been given all of these supernatural gifts like Padre Pio of Pietrelcina.

Padre Pio has accomplished deeds that are beyond the scope of ordinary mortals, and these are borne witness to daily from every corner of the earth. I have reported upon many of these facts in my other books: "Per la Storia," "Fatti Nuova," "Fino alla Meta," so that here I shall only sketch a few, as I have limited myself as to space.

Before beginning my story, I wish to make the following statement: Only after his death, will our children and grand-children be in a position to say who Padre Pio is; for then he will undergo his canonical trial; in the meantime we, as obe-dient children of Holy Mother Church, follow her teachings and abide by her laws.

The spiritual children of Padre Pio, scattered all over the world, know well who he is, it would be well for those who do not know him to learn to do so, for they would obtain the help of a spiritual guide for the rest of their lives.

Whoever receives the grace of conversion will experience the very same joys that were granted to me; for he will see how the spirit can conquer the flesh, how love can triumph over hate, and faith over incredulity. He will realize that eternal truth banishes doubt and despair, and he will know that all human knowledge pales before the crucifix; for we are penetrated by a divine fire that never leaves us, but draws us up into the knowledge and the presence of God. We know that we shall reap the fruit of our work in God's vineyard when He calls us to Himself.

The love that his spiritual children feel for Padre Pio is not fanaticism, but rather a most humble respect for one who will

14

bring them nearer to Almighty God. They are crusaders of faith and love, for they are committed to spread the one and the other among those who are lacking in both, and this they do in the name of God and of their spiritual father.

Padre Pio wishes that all of his children should consider themselves brothers, should banish all hate forever in the flame of God's love, and that they may come to him with such a deep and sincere longing for perfection that he can bring them before God restored to their baptismal innocence.

Let us follow him then, this chosen one, who takes upon himself reparation for all of the evil that we have committed, and just as he imitates Our Lord and offers all of himself to God, we can imitate him and advance far along in the spiritual life.

THE GIFT OF PERFUME

Among the many gifts that God has bestowed upon Padre Pio one of the most remarkable is certainly that of his perfume.

Very many people claim that they have experienced this perfume of the Padre's, even at great distances; they describe it as similar to that which is noticed when one comes near to him and to his stigmatized hands and even to his clothes and objects that have been touched by him.

It is important to note that the Father reveals himself to different people in a different manner; each perfume has its own significance and is a proof that he has heard their prayer. It comes as a warning to proceed with or to desist from some action, or to pray or to hope. It is sometimes very distinct and sometimes faint; it reminds one of roses or violets or lilies; at times of incense, at others of carbolic acid or even of tobacco.

It is almost impossible to classify these different types of perfume or to explain their significance, but it is known and attested by the Church that all through her history there have been holy people who have been gifted in this mysterious way either during life or even after death.

St. Joseph of Cupertino exuded from his person a sweet and delicate perfume, and no one could ever give a reason for it; his clothes were impregnated with it and it clung to his cell for twelve years after his death.

A very special perfume came from the tombs of St. Anthony of Padua and of St. Dominic Guzman among others, and in all cases it had the quality of pleasing even those who disliked any perfume.

Professor Romanelli visited Padre Pio five times, and at fiirst was surprised that the Father should use scent; he realized later the true significance of this spiritual manifestation and his surprise was changed to profound admiration during the fifteen months of his medical observations.

This perfume is part of his biolocation and in a way a proof that Our Lord dwells in him and he in Our Lord.

As a general rule, the perfume is first noticed when one is on one's way to Padre Pio or just after having left him; but what is more extraordinary is the fact that it is often noticed in far distant lands, such as Africa, America or Asia. This can not be explained by autosuggestion, as it is impossible so to create odor that will be smelled by a group of people at the same time, but which suggests to each one something as different as lilies, or tobacco or even carbolic acid.

Perfume is always caused by an emanation from an object or person; it reaches the nostrils of the one who perceives it, and he in turn recognizes it as characteristic of the object or person from which it comes.

Padre Pio's perfume has a real meaning to his spiritual children, it proves to them that he is following them from afar and is warning, guiding and supporting them, that he is giving them specific advice to do some definite thing or not to do it.

THE GIFT OF CONVERSION

Padre Pio will go down in history as one who knew how to convert.

It is impossible to know the names of all those who have been converted by him or to describe all of the spiritual transformations he has effected upon the souls of his visitors.

I shall mention only a few names; but each of these has behind it an unwritten volume of suffering and joy, and if any of it has been brought to light, the description was only a pale shadow of what had been experienced.

Among the most spectacular conversions were Festa, a lawyer of Genoa, and cousin of the Doctor Festa who examined the Father; Di Maggio di Partinico, also a lawyer; Signora Luisa Vairo; the writer Checcacci of Genoa, the Russian Colonel Caterinitch; the sculptor Francesco Messina; then there is Father Pio of the Trinitarians, as well as Pitigrilli and many others.

Among all of the gifts that God has showered on Padre Pio, I consider that this one is even greater than the healing of the sick and infirm, for in the latter a material change takes place that modifies a situation only for the time being, whereas conversion brings about a spiritual regeneration that has almost always a permanent quality, that is, it lasts for eternity.

I have only mentioned a few names, and there are thousands of others; many of these have never been willing to sign a statement or send in a report, either from false modesty or conventionality or perhaps even because of not correctly evaluating the grace they have received. We must not forget that whoever has received absolution after confession is returned to a state of grace even after years of sinful life, just as though he had been newly baptized.

Since names without facts are a dead letter to the average reader, I shall make a few rapid sketches of particular cases.

A very dear friend of mine, the late Ferruccio Caponetti who was also once a Mason, then a convert as I was, wrote to me in November 1931:

"My dear Alberto, the Lord has infinite ways! You crossed my path, you showed me the right road, I took heed and climbed up the steep slope of Monte Gargano where I found the Master; he received me with joy because he saw that I was blind, and he listened smiling to the doubts that were in my mind. With simple words but with most profound wisdom he demolished one by one all of the theories that filled my mind, and I found myself without arguments to oppose him; he stripped my soul bare and by showing me Our Lord's sublime teaching he reopened the eyes of my soul; I was able to see the true light, my inmost heart was touched and I knew the meaning of Faith.

"I now enjoy true peace of soul, I now know the true God. For this I am grateful to you, for I owe you so much, and to Padre Pio I owe everything!"

A lawyer from Genoa, a cousin of Doctor Festa of Rome, persuaded that his cousin was in a state of exaltation, decided to go incognito to Padre Pio.

As soon as the Father laid eyes on him he exclaimed: "What are you doing here? You are a Mason!" This was followed by verbal blows and counter-blows which all ended in the lawyer kneeling down in front of the humble friar who had converted him.

Meditation before Mass

Stigmata of Padre Pio in 1918

Baptizing

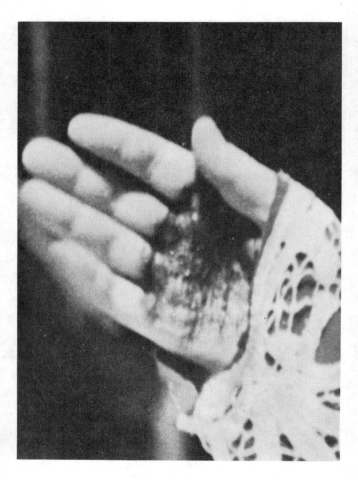

Stigmatized Right Hand

Ecce Agnus Dei

Padre Pio as Deacon

Blessing the Host

Last Blessing

On his return to Genoa he wrote a long letter to his cousin in Rome. Among other things he said: "Thanks! You have opened up a way for me which I shall follow. I can not tell you about it in writing, because it is all impossible to describe. I can only say that I have come home with a deep sense of peace in my soul, I long for silence so that nothing may disturb my spirit."

He later became a stretcher-bearer following the sick pilgrims who traveled to Lourdes. He was received by his Holiness Benedict XV, who said to him: "Padre Pio is truly a man of God. Take on the task of making him better known, he is not appreciated by all as he deserves."

*　　*　　*

Professor G. Felice Checcacci of Genoa, a writer well known in Italy, who lived for upward of forty years in the Orient, and had the opportunity to study a great variety of religions, he read a book of mine a few years ago and wrote me the following: "You are lucky to be able to go so often to see Padre Pio! What peace you must feel in your soul! Please embrace him humbly for me." He then went on to tell me about his conversion and said: "I must admit that I had not been inside of a church out of devotion for over forty years. I obeyed, however, and as I prayed I heard a voice within me that whispered 'Faith can not be discussed; you must either shut your eyes and accept it at the same time acknowledging the inadequacy of the human mind when confronted with a mystery, or you will have to give it up. There is no middle way. It is for you to choose.' From that day I chose the road I would follow, and I owe my return to the religion of my forefathers to Padre Pio.

"From that time I realized all of the beauty that exists in Christian charity, and the selfishness and indifference to human suffering by Asiatic religions founded on the doctrine of fatalism and reincarnation."

*   *   *

One day a poor man came with a very sick child; he had consulted a number of doctors and had spent much money in the search of a cure. He brought him to the Padre while he was still feverish, hoping for a miracle.

When he entered the confessional Padre Pio chased him away with these words: "What are you doing in front of God's tribunal if you don't believe? Go! Go away! You are a communist!"

The man went back to his lodgings with the intention of taking his child home, but a professor who happened to be there persuaded him to return to the Father and confess his sins, at the same time renouncing the evil teachings of Moscow. In the afternoon he returned to the monastery Church with the intention of going to confession. As soon as he saw the Father he threw himself weeping at his feet, unable to utter a word.

Padre Pio raised him up from the ground and said: "Now that's the way! A good scrubbing is what you need, but you have to have the will to be clean. You have done the right thing and your son will get well. Now come to confession." The poor man wept during his confession, being very deeply moved. The child was cured physically just as his father was cured spiritually.

*   *   *

CURES

The number of people who have come to Padre Pio to beg for his prayers are legion; they have come to him suffering from every sort of illness, such as advanced conditions of cancer, tuberculosis of the lungs or of the bones, maladies

28

that had been pronounced chronic or incurable by medical science. He is begged by all to pray God for the cure of their bodily ills, and ultimately for good of their souls.

Whenever the Father accomplishes one of these astonishing cures he says: "God has granted you this grace, address your thanks to Him and not to me!" Although he is aware of his power, he never allows it to encroach upon his humility.

The average reader insists upon deeds rather than words; let me assure him that the Father has accomplished more amazing deeds than could possibly be imagined. I do not know all of them, by any means, and in many cases I am not at liberty to record them with the names and addresses of the people involved. It is therefor difficult to describe in a few words that which amply deserves a long and detailed account.

I shall do the best I can with the small space available and from among many others I shall mention the one case I have followed most closely, the cure of Signorina Maria Panisi, who was born in New York and now lives in Pietrel-cina.

Maria Panisi was suffering from tuberculosis, and had been pronounced incurable by several well-known doctors, among others Dr. Moscato of the University of Naples, who had declared to the girl's father in 1923 that: "By the time the trees lose their leaves your daughter will have passed on to a better life."

This happened thirty years ago, and Maria Panisi now lives in the little village where Padre Pio was born. The leaves have fallen thirty times, but she continues to feel perfectly well.

How did this happen? It was very simple: the father of the girl, who came from the same village as Padre Pio, brought her to San Giovanni. The Padre patted her gently on the shoulder with his hand and said: "What do you mean by saying you are sick? Your lungs are made of steel!" And from that day Maria Panisi had no more hemorrhages and was as well as any girl of her age.

*　　*　　*

A Countess Baiocci of Gavina who lived in Rome was suffering from an unknown disease. She consulted many doctors and was finally advised by Dr. Giorgio Festa to go to San Giovanni Rotondo. The day after her arrival she was completely cured.

*　　*　　*

A young lady from Bologna who is still living had been warned by an eminent physician that one of her bones could never knit, as she had broken it too long ago. She was completely cured the first time she followed Padre Pio's instructions and this happened on the feast of St. Francis.

*　　*　　*

A military chaplain told me that in a hospital that receives 37,000 patients in the course of two years, only fifty-three of them had died, and he attributed this fact to his having blessed each one of the wounded with a crucifix that had been blessed by Padre Pio. Later on he had two ships torpedoed under him and in both cases his life was saved.

*　　*　　*

At Bagnoreggio near Viterbo a child suffering from meningitis was left in a spastic condition and sent away from the hospital as incurable. Padre Pio's prayers cured him.

*　　*　　*

In Ragusa a seven months old infant was cured of a convulsive cough owing to the great faith of her parents in Padre Pio who obtained her cure through his prayers. This was confirmed by Dr. Tagliaferri, a well-known pediatrician.

*　　*　　*

A boy by the name of Fernander of Hamrun in Malta was suddenly stricken with a high fever; it was diagnosed by blood test as Malta or Mediterranean fever. Various doctors in consultation decided to immobilize his knee joint in a plaster cast fearing that his leg would be permanently deformed.

The child's mother, who was a spiritual child of Padre Pio, sent him a telegram begging for prayers. She received an answer from San Giovanni Rotondo which said: "Padre Pio blesses and prays." The doctors noticed a distinct improvement on their next visit, the idea of the plaster cast was given up, and a few days later the boy had completely recovered.

* * *

At San Felice a Cancello, Naples, a young woman by the name of Nicoletta Mazzone was dying of a complication of bronchial complaints in the course of which she had even lost the power of speech. Her agonized father traveled to San Giovanni Rotondo to beg for a cure. Padre Pio smiled when he said to him: "Go back home and be glad, for the Madonna delle Grazie will cure your child." Mazzone did not accept this statement, but implored the Father anew, at which he answered, though no longer smiling: "Man of little faith! I repeat to you, go home and rejoice, for the Madonna delle Grazie will cure her!"

On his return to his village he was met by his wife and sister who joyfully announced to him that the dying girl had spoken, and had said that she was hungry. From that day on she grew better and eventually was completely cured.

I was told of this by the uncle of the young lady, a Mr. F. Flamman of 6009 8th Avenue, Brooklyn, New York.

* * *

A woman from Pesaro, the wife of a workman, brought her deaf and dumb child to Padre Pio. He cured her instantly. In an outburst of gratitude the woman took a gold chain from

31

the child's neck, the only object of value that she owned, and gave it to Padre Pio for the Virgin. When she reached home she told everything to her husband who flew into a rage at the offering she had made to the Father: he said that she should have chosen some other article rather than the gift that he himself had made to his daughter.

The next morning they found the chain on the bed table.

* * *

The Reverend Emilio Secchi, parish priest of Avandrace, Cagliari, told me the following story in 1947: the head of the Girl's Protective Association (name not given) came down with typhoid and was taken in all haste to the local hospital for infectious diseases.

As it was impossible for a letter to travel from Avandrace to San Giovanni Rotondo in less than several days, the father of the patient sent a telegram to Padre Pio, begging him to pray for the speedy recovery of his daughter, whose presence was urgently needed in carrying on the work of the parish, and who was impossible to replace.

The young woman was only allowed to remain for twenty-four hours in the hospital, she was sent home to die, as there was no hope of her recovery.

However, she did recover. Padre Pio on receiving the telegram asked the Lord to restore her to perfect health. The priest who sent me the story added that he had no hesitation in attributing the cure of this person to the prayers of Padre Pio.

I shall close with the extraordinary story of Wanda Sari of Treviso who was suffering from a grievous malady and in great pain. The doctors had given her but a few hours to live, when a friend showed her a photograph of Padre Pio; she begged him with all her might for a cure, and all of a sudden her pains disappeared. She later went to San Giovanni Rotondo to thank the Padre, and on her way there came to see me. I had in my possession a photograph which had been sent to me at the time of her illness; in it she looked completely emancipated. I saw before me now a fine, healthy child whose angelic expression helped me to see the reason for the miracle.

* * *

Padre Pio has been blessed with a gift that he shares with a number of saints who have been honored by our Holy Mother the Church, namely the power to be in several places at once. It has often been noticed that when someone has been recommended to the prayers of Padre Pio, his face undergoes a change and his eyes become luminous while at the same time he seems to murmur a prayer. It is as though he were partly absent, and had gone to the side of the person who needed him. He does in fact not only go from one place to another, but he is able to project his voice and also his perfume.

* * *

This supernatural gift can be proven by various known facts. In my book "Fino alla Meta" I tell of a young aviator who was attached to a fighter squadron in the last war.

One day the lieutenant started off on a mission, and discovered right away that his plane was about to catch fire. He consulted his commanding officer by radio, who told him that if he could not put out the blaze he was to bail out of the plane with his parachute. All of his efforts were in vain so he jumped, but the parachute failed to open. He would have been killed had not a friar caught him in his arms and carried him to earth.

That evening he told his story to his commanding officer who did not believe a word of it, but gave him a short leave in order to recover from the shock of the experience.

When he reached home he told his tale to his mother. "Why it was Padre Pio," she said "I prayed to him so hard for you!"

and she showed him a picture of the Padre. Her son exclaimed: "Mother! That is the same man!"

The young soldier went to San Giovanni Rotondo to express his gratitude. Padre Pio said to him: "That was not the only time I saved you. At Monastir when your plane had been hit, I made it glide safely to earth." Which had actually happened.

*   *   *

A certain prelate went to Rome for the beatification of St. Teresa of the Child Jesus. Wishing to pray at the tomb of His Holiness St. Pius X, he asked to have the gate of the crypt opened for him. What was his astonishment when he saw a Capuchin praying there, inside of the enclosure. When he had finished his prayers he turned to speak to the friar but he had vanished. He found out later by description that he had seen Padre Pio.

*   *   *

A certain sick woman in Borgomanero was visited by the Padre through bilocation; she begged him to leave her some remembrance of his visit, at which he placed his wounded hand on the edge of her bed. Five bloodstains in the form of crosses remained upon the sheet, a fact that needs no explanation.

*   *   *

What has always seemed to me the most impressive of all the astonishing facts about Padre Pio is the story of Monsignor Fernando Damiani, the Vicar General of Salto, Uruguay. His brother was the famous baritone, Victor Damiani of the "Colon" of Buenos Aires. Padre Pio had at one time cured the prelate of a cancer of the stomach, which had made them great friends over the years. Some time later Msgr. Damiani returned to Italy and went to see Padre Pio. He spoke with some feeling of his desire to stay in Italy, his native land, as he was now advanced in years. Padre Pio advised him to go back to Uruguay, as it was not time yet for his number to be called; he also promised him that he would visit him at the time of his death. The Monsignor then left for South America.

For the celebration of the twenty-fifth anniversary of the ordination of His Excellency Bishop Alfredo Viola of Salto, Uruguay, Msgr. Damiani joined the throng of distinguished ecclesiastics who came from all over South America for the occasion. He, in his capacity of Vicar General was expected to be present at all the ceremonies but an attack of angina pectoris prevented him from doing this and he died, being assisted at the end not only by a number of bishops but by Padre Pio himself, who kept his promise. Msgr. Damiani was able to scribble a note to that effect with the words: "Padre Pio came."

Two important churchmen confirmed this, and when they came to Italy they got Padre Pio to admit that it was true.

* * *

The appearance of Padre Pio to young Giacomo Calice of the Foreign Legion is also noteworthy. One night when he was standing guard at an advance outpost and feeling miserably frightened by the solitude of the desert, a man appeared full of reassurance and told him to follow him. He led him to the coast where he found a raft that took him to Marseilles, and from thence he got to Corsica, his native land.

Signor Pietro Calice, the boy's father, had gone to Padre Pio some time before and had begged him to bring about the return of his son to their home. The Padre promised him that the sheep would return to the fold provided that he prayed God with great love and faith. And all this came about. When the father showed his son a picture of Padre Pio, he said to him: "That is the man who led me out of the desert!"

I could go on with no end of such stories, but I ask the reader to look in the books I have mentioned above, where they will be found in greater detail.

DISCERNMENT OF SPIRITS

Whoever has used the powers of the soul and has succeeded in raising himself up, even for an instant, above the "burden of his flesh," and lifted his spirit to God, will have experienced something that is unknown to the great majority of the human race.

By reading the lives of the saints we learn that the mystical life enhances all of the senses, especially that of sight, thereby making the saint more observant in matters that concern his walk of life. The Blessed Anna Maria Taig was very close to Padre Pio in this. Skeptics, even among the clergy, who scorn those who believe that Padre Pio can read consciences and be aware of events that are taking place far away from him, either in the past or in the future, must be confounded by what has been proved again and again.

St. Joseph of Cupertino could recognize carnal sins by the smell of his penitents. Padre Pio, just looking at a man said: "Oh Genoese, you have a dirty face!" by which he was referring to the condition of his soul.

* * *

To a young woman the Padre said: "If you have had the courage to imitate Mary Magdalen in her sins, have the courage to imitate her penance!"

* * *

A woman driver who had blasphemed, and did not confess her sin, was reminded by him of the circumstances of her transgression.

* * *

Someone had asked him during the elevation to obtain for him a certain favor, and repeated the request during an interview. He said: "Do you think I am deaf? There is no need to repeat things twice!"

* * *

A Swiss priest presented him with an unopened letter, Padre Pio said "This is the answer." And he gave him a written answer to his letter that had not been unsealed.

* * *

A French abbot, Father Benoit, had been puzzled for some time by a problem that he was unable to solve. As he was leaving Padre Pio who sensed that he was going away unsatisfied, he asked him for his breviary and on it he wrote the answer to the problem. It is interesting to note that the abbot had never mentioned what was preoccupying him, but Padre Pio was able to detect it and give him a proof of his discernment.

* * *

Two girls came to him who had promised their father not to kiss Padre Pio's hand for fear of infection. "Pay attention to your father's advice!" he said to them as they approached him.

* * *

Mrs. Mary Forster of Hazelton, New York received her passport which was to enable her to rejoin her husband in Europe, after it had been refused her by the State Department. She never knew how it came through, but she and her children were able to sail and were safely brought through a difficult trip. Padre Pio had sent her word that she was not to worry, that he would pray that all would go well with them and would assist them on their journey.

Mrs. Forster and her husband, an engineer, came to see me with their two children in Bologna when they came to Italy to thank Padre Pio.

GIFT OF PROPHECY

God, having given His servant the gift of seeing into the past and the present, has certainly given him the faculty of seeing into the future. Of this there are innumerable proofs. Many of these predictions have been verified because of the short space of time involved, others will not be proven correct until a long time hence. Is it not a gift of prophecy when the Padre promises a cure to a person whose case has been pronounced desperate? Or to someone who is in urgent need of help in some emergency? How can one explain his predictions of the sex of an unborn infant? The date of a conversion? A death? . . . . . Padre Pio once told a young man that he would be dead by a certain day and that he must prepare his soul; it happened as he said.

* * *

During the last war the Father promised that not a single bomb would fall upon San Giovanni Rotondo, and none did. Some people may say that it was a question of chance, but many aviators have declared that when they flew over San Giovanni they could not release their bombs.

* * *

During the earthquake at Valnure, the water supply was destroyed in Pietrelcina and the inhabitants were in despair, not being able to water their cattle. They came to Padre Pio who asked them to show him a map of the region where the new monastery was being built, and the work was at a standstill owing to the lack of water. He put his finger on a certain spot and said "Dig a well five meters from here and you will find all the water you want." Not even the divining rods had succeeded in finding any, but Padre Pio did.

To a captain of Carabinieri he prophesied that he would have a son and to someone who wished for a daughter after having had five sons, he said: "It will be a little girl." And it was.

*   *   *

Did not Padre Pio say that the Blessed Virgin would save Italy? That the Casa Sollievo della Sofferenza would be built? That a woman would have a child after eight years of marriage without one? And I could go on.

At times the Father states a fact in the clearest terms, at others he is almost sybilline and oracular. This generally depends upon the spiritual state of the person concerned. It would be too easy to say: "If I don't get what I want, I'll do as I please!" You can be sure that this will never happen.

*   *   *

I have attempted to give you some idea of this wonderful man of God. Before closing I feel that I should tell you something of his Mass and of his manner of hearing confessions.

PADRE PIO'S MASS

The impressions made by a visit to Padre Pio are various, but what moves people most is his Mass, or rather the manner in which he renews the Passion of Our Lord.

When the hour of Mass approaches, all faces are turned toward the sacristy from which the Padre will come, seeming to walk painfully on his pierced feet. We feel that grace itself is approaching us, forcing us to bend our knees.

It is difficult and indeed nearly impossible to describe the Mass of Padre Pio. Many have tried without too much success. Padre Pio is not an ordinary priest, but a creature in pain who renews the Passion of Christ, with the devotion and radiance of one who is inspired by God.

After he steps to the altar and makes the Sign of the Cross, the Padre's face is transfigured, and he seems like a creature who becomes one with his Creator. Suffering shines through his features, and all can see the painful contractions of his body, especially when he leans on the altar and genuflects, as though he bore the weight of the cross; in the meantime tears roll down his cheeks and from his mouth come words of prayer, of supplication for pardon, of love for his Lord of whom he seems to become a perfect replica.

None of those present notice the passage of time; it takes him about one hour and a half to say his Mass, but the attention of all is riveted on every gesture, movement and expression of the celebrant. At the sound of the word "Credo" pronounced with such tremendous conviction, there is a great wave of emotion through the throng, and the most recalcitrant of sinners is carried along as on a stream that is bringing him to the confessional and the renunciation of his old way of life.

CONFESSION

Many writers on Padre Pio, like myself, have said that he is absolutely unique as a confessor. What distinguishes him from others is his faculty of bringing to the mind of his penitent certain sins that he wishes him to confess. He sometimes mentions these faults himself, especially when he sees that the penitent, although well prepared, is so bewildered in his presence that he is unable to say anything at all. He sometimes reminds him of some sin that he has neglected to mention in previous confessions.

The first time that I went to confession to him was in November 1930. "Father" I said, "I have never had faith, but I have always been honest. Even when . . . " And he told me things that no mortal could have known, that I had forgotten, or not mentioned as they did not seem to me to be important.

Frederico Abresch, a convert from Protestantism was made to realize that in his preceding confessions he had withheld some grave faults, and to prove to him that he knew all about it the Father asked him when he had last made a good confession. Abresch could not remember, so the Padre said: "The last time that you made a good confession was on your honeymoon." And this was really so.

*　　*　　*

Padre Pio can tell you exactly how many times you have missed Mass, how many promises have been broken, the number of faults willfully committed, the mortal sins omitted in confession, and the venial sins that must never be committed again.

If he is sometimes severe it is because many people approach the confessional lightly, without giving the sacrament its true importance; or what annoys him more is when people come to him merely to test his apparent omniscience. I do not advise anyone to attempt this, for besides offending the Padre, who is the intermediary between man and God, and whose role is to help us to recover our state of grace, it causes a grave offense to Almighty God.

It is only after having received absolution that the penitent can ask the Father for that thing that he so much desires. It is then that the Father promises to pray: for the recovery of someone dear to you —
- for a successful operation
- that a child presumed lost may return safely
- for a boy or a girl as yet unborn
- for the assurance that some definite event will come about or not
- for a successful examination

When Padre Pio leaves the confessional his step is slower and he looks very tired; it is as though in addition to his own cross, he were bearing those of the souls that he has brought back to God.

When he absolves, Padre Pio gives the penitent a definite number of short prayers to say, and these must often be recited over a period of months. He knows the irresistible force of prayer, and that it is the key to the Heart of Our Lord, the link which binds the creature to the Creator, that makes him a slave to Divine Love.

It is also well to know that when the Father has bought a soul by means of his suffering, he does not allow Satan to recapture it, for he is always at hand to guide, to support and to help it in every circumstance that may arise. It was thus that he reassured a lawyer from Rome who was fearful lest he return to his former sinful ways: "My son," he said, "pray without ceasing and never leave off, and you can be sure that when I have rescued a soul I never let it fall again."

* * *

All those who know Padre Pio have heard him tell funny stories; indeed he must have a whole anthology of them in his head. His answers are full of humor and he likes a joke. On my last visit to him in April 1954, (it was my thirty-fifth) he was in the garden listening to the complaints of some of his spiritual sons. Suddenly he smiled and said: "None of you are happy, only we monks are happy, do you know why?" Then he made the sign of the cross and said: "We have no debts, we have no credit, we have no wives, nor any children . . . and so be it!"

* * *

And I could go on forever!

CASA SOLLIEVO DELLA SOFFERENZA
(The House for the Relief of Suffering)

Before ending this very short profile of Padre Pio, I think

42

it is in order to say a few words about the "Casa Sollievo della Sofferenza," the magnificent hospital that Padre Pio built at San Giovanni Rotondo in the Province of Foggia, for the sick of Monte Gargano where no hospital existed, as well as for the suffering people of all Italy who may come to see him.

This imposing structure takes in people of all races, creeds or political persuasion.

How did this ambitious plan arise? On the evening of the 9th of January 1940, the Padre said to three of his spiritual sons: "Our Lord suffers in every creature who is ill." And then, suddenly taking from his pocket a small gold coin that he had received as a gift, he said "I wish to make the first contribution toward the building of a hospital."

The idea took hold immediately and the contributions began to pour in. At first they consisted mostly in the small change from a blind man, or the pennies from some child's bank; but in 1947 Miss Barbara Ward, now Mrs. Jackson, brought 250 million lire to the Casa di Sollievo from UNRRA funds.

The hospital is very large and is provided with all of the most modern equipment of every description, including a department of radio-therapy which is perhaps the best in the world. Signor Lupi of Pescara was the architect and engineer, and is well known for his many important buildings.

The director of the Casa di Sollievo was the late Dr. Guglielo Sanguinetti, once also an atheist, who left his practice and his clinic in Florence to support the work of the Padre.

A very big statue of St. Francis of Assisi dominates the hospital; it is twenty feet high and was made by a native artist who like Cimabue and Andrea del Sarto, was once a shepherd and modeled little figures out of clay as he watched his sheep. His name is Antonio Berti and he now teaches in the Accademia delle Belle Arti in Florence.

Above the hospital is a landing platform for the helicopters that are used to transport the patients who come from a distance. From there shines the "Beacon of Love" whose light is visible at a great distance and reminds travelers at night of Padre Pio and how he serves God on Monte Gargano.

Padre Pio celebrated the 50th anniversary of his stigmata on September 20, 1968. Three days later, on September 23, 1968 he passed away. The present volume is kept in print to meet the widespread interest in his life and work.

Holy Eucharist—Our All. *Etlin* 3.00
Glories of Divine Grace. *Fr. Scheeben* 18.00
Saint Michael and the Angels. *Approved Sources* 9.00
Dolorous Passion of Our Lord. *Anne C. Emmerich* 18.00
Our Lady of Fatima's Peace Plan from Heaven. *Booklet* 1.00
Three Ways of the Spiritual Life. *Garrigou-Lagrange* 7.00
Mystical Evolution. 2 Vols. *Fr. Arintero, O.P.* 42.00
St. Catherine Labouré of the Mirac. Medal. *Fr. Dirvin* 16.50
Manual of Practical Devotion to St. Joseph. *Patrignani* 17.50
The Active Catholic. *Fr. Palau* 9.00
Ven. Jacinta Marto of Fatima. *Cirrincione* 3.00
Reign of Christ the King. *Davies* 2.00
St. Teresa of Ávila. *William Thomas Walsh* 24.00
Isabella of Spain—The Last Crusader. *Wm. T. Walsh* 24.00
Characters of the Inquisition. *Wm. T. Walsh* 16.50
Blood-Drenched Altars—Cath. Comment. Hist. Mexico 21.50
Self-Abandonment to Divine Providence. *de Caussade* 22.50
Way of the Cross. *Liguorian* 1.50
Way of the Cross. *Franciscan* 1.50
Modern Saints—Their Lives & Faces, Bk. 1. *Ann Ball* 21.00
Modern Saints—Their Lives & Faces, Bk. 2. *Ann Ball* 23.00
Divine Favors Granted to St. Joseph. *Pere Binet* 7.50
St. Joseph Cafasso—Priest of the Gallows. *St. J. Bosco* 6.00
Catechism of the Council of Trent. *McHugh/Callan* 27.50
Why Squander Illness? *Frs. Rumble & Carty* 4.00
Fatima—The Great Sign. *Francis Johnston* 12.00
Heliotropium—Conformity of Human Will to Divine 15.00
Charity for the Suffering Souls. *Fr. John Nageleisen* 18.00
Devotion to the Sacred Heart of Jesus. *Verheylezoon* 16.50
Sermons on Prayer. *St. Francis de Sales* 7.00
Sermons on Our Lady. *St. Francis de Sales* 15.00
Sermons for Lent. *St. Francis de Sales* 15.00
Fundamentals of Catholic Dogma. *Ott* 27.50
Litany of the Blessed Virgin Mary. (100 cards) 5.00
Who Is Padre Pio? *Radio Replies Press* 3.00
Child's Bible History. *Knecht* 7.00
St. Anthony—The Wonder Worker of Padua. *Stoddard* 7.00
The Precious Blood. *Fr. Faber* 16.50
The Holy Shroud & Four Visions. *Fr. O'Connell* 3.50
Clean Love in Courtship. *Fr. Lawrence Lovasik* 4.50
The Secret of the Rosary. *St. Louis De Montfort* 5.00

At your Bookdealer or direct from the Publisher.
Call Toll Free 1-800-437-5876

Prices subject to change.